ROLLER DERBY

By Demi Jackson

Please visit our website, www.garethstevens.com. For a free color catalog of all our high-quality books, call toll free 1-800-542-2595 or fax 1-877-542-2596.

Jackson, Demi.
  Roller derby / Demi Jackson.
    pages cm. — (Daredevil sports)
  Includes bibliographical references and index.
  ISBN 978-1-4824-2998-5 (pbk.)
  ISBN 978-1-4824-2997-8 (6 pack)
  ISBN 978-1-4824-2999-2 (library binding)
  1. Roller derby—Juvenile literature. I. Title.
  GV859.6.J34 2016
  796.21—dc23
                                        2015011019

First Edition

Published in 2016 by
Gareth Stevens Publishing
111 East 14th Street, Suite 349
New York, NY 10003

Designer: Samantha DeMartin
Editor: Kristen Rajczak

Photo credits: Cover, pp. 1, 7 Robert Cianflone/Getty Images Sport/Getty Images; pp. 5, 11, 19, 21, 23 (main) Paul J. Richards/AFP/Getty Images; p. 9 George Skadding/The LIFE Picture Collection/Getty Images; p. 13 Sergei Bachlakov/Shutterstock.com; p. 15 Shirlaine Forrest/WireImage/Getty Images; p. 23 (inset) Annette Shaff/Shutterstock.com; p. 25 Shirlaine Forrest/Getty Images Sport/Getty Images; p. 27 Stan Honda/AFP/Getty Images; p. 29 Hagen Hopkins/Getty Images Entertainment/Getty Images.

Printed in the United States of America

CPSIA compliance information: Batch #CS15GS: For further information contact Gareth Stevens, New York, New York at 1-800-542-2595.

CONTENTS

HARD-HITTING SPORT

Imagine roller-skating around a roller rink as fast as you can. You try to skate around someone, and she throws her shoulder into your chest to stop you. Do you fall, or do you slip by her?

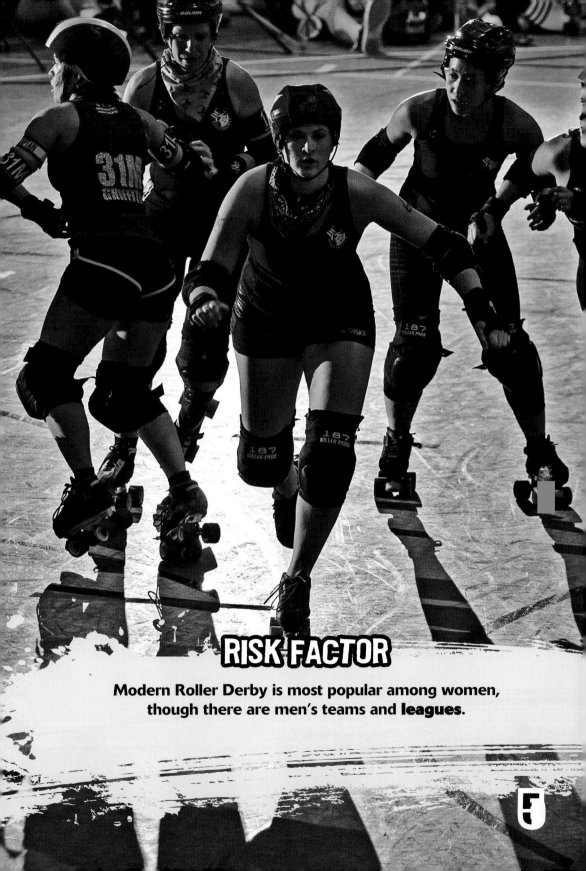

RISK FACTOR

Modern Roller Derby is most popular among women, though there are men's teams and leagues.

Roller Derby is a sport in which two teams roller-skate around an oval track, trying to score the most points. Each team has five skaters on the track at a time during a game, or bout.

RISK FACTOR

Roller Derby is a full-contact sport. That means skaters can—and do—push, pull, and hit one another!

HOW IT STARTED

Roller Derby started as a long, hard roller-skating **event** around 1935. The crowd loved when two skaters ran into each other! Soon, the sport changed to make these hits part of the event. Roller Derby stayed popular until the 1970s.

RISK FACTOR

Early Roller Derby events took place on banked tracks, which are higher on the outside.

BACK IN ACTION!

Roller Derby teams were never totally gone. But it was a league that formed in Austin, Texas, in 2001 that restarted interest in Roller Derby, especially among women. Today, there are more than 30 leagues across the United States.

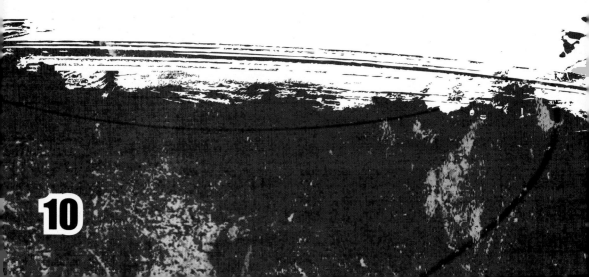

RISK FACTOR

Most Roller Derby leagues today play on flat tracks.
This allows bouts to happen just about anywhere,
including at existing roller rinks!

BOUTS AND PLAYERS

Each Roller Derby bout has two 30-minute halves. Within those halves are an unlimited number of jams, or races, that last up to 2 minutes each. Each team has five players on the track at a time: the jammer, the pivot, and blockers.

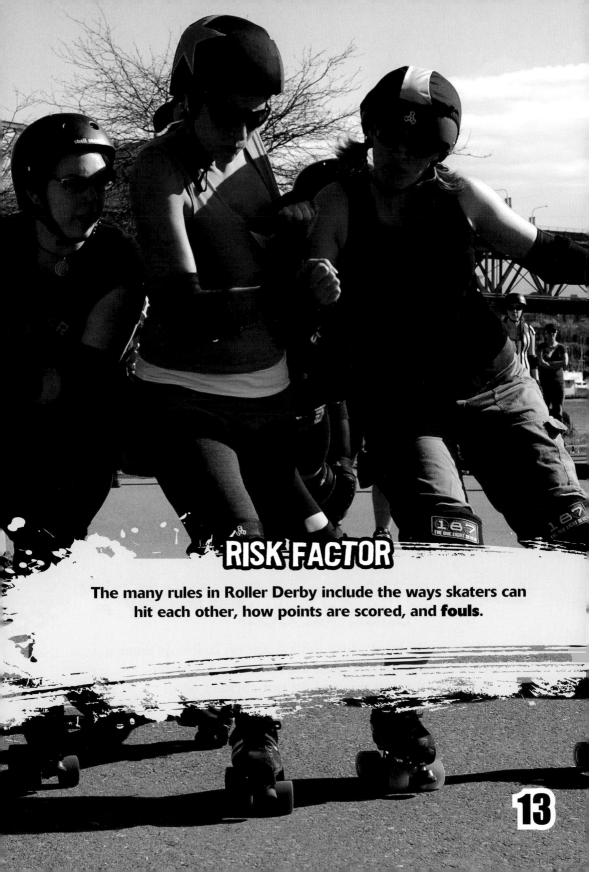

RISK FACTOR

The many rules in Roller Derby include the ways skaters can hit each other, how points are scored, and **fouls**.

The jammer's job is to score points. The blockers try to stop the other team's jammer and help their jammer through the crowd of skaters. The pivot calls plays and **paces** her team. The pivot also acts as another blocker.

RISK FACTOR

Jammers wear a helmet cover with a star on it. Pivots wear a helmet cover with stripes. Blockers have a blank helmet—though they might put stickers on it!

15

LET'S JAM!

When a jam starts, both teams'
pivots and blockers—or the
pack—line up together behind
the start line. The jammers line up
behind them. The pack starts to
skate at the first whistle. The
second whistle means the jammers
can start.

ROLLER DERBY
STARTING POSITIONS

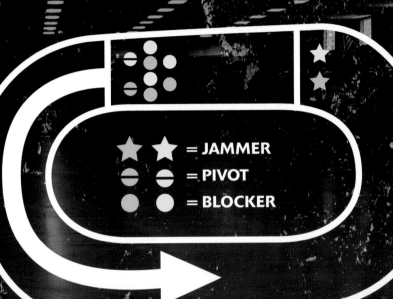

= JAMMER
= PIVOT
= BLOCKER

RISK FACTOR

The main Roller Derby organization is the Women's Flat Track Derby Association (WFTDA).

The first jammer to catch up to the pack and make it through them without a foul is the lead jammer. She can call off the jam at any time. If there's no lead jammer, the jam will last the full 2 minutes.

RISK FACTOR

Teams can switch skaters, or substitute, between jams.

No points are scored on the jammers' first lap. For each player of the other team a jammer passes on the rest of the laps, her team gets a point. Of course, the blockers are using their bodies to slow or stop the other team's jammer at the same time!

RISK FACTOR

The many **referees** in Roller Derby each have a certain part of the jam to watch, such as counting the lead jammer's points or making sure the blockers are following the rules.

DERBY GEAR

Since Roller Derby is a fast-paced, full-contact sport, safety gear is very important. Each skater needs to wear a helmet that fits well. The best kind for Roller Derby is plastic with foam inside. It can withstand big hits or many smaller ones.

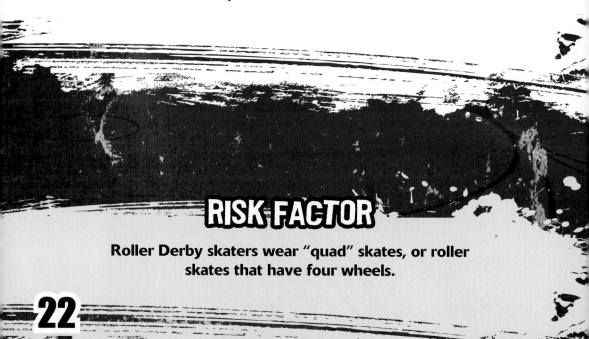

RISK FACTOR

Roller Derby skaters wear "quad" skates, or roller skates that have four wheels.

quad skates

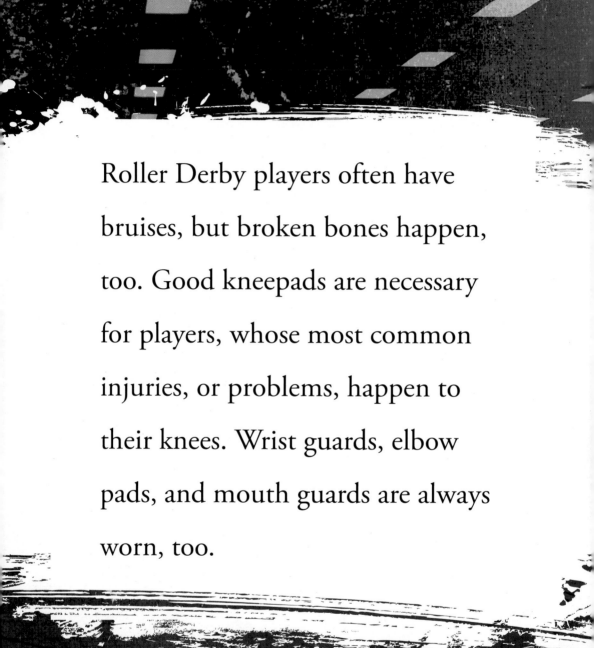

Roller Derby players often have bruises, but broken bones happen, too. Good kneepads are necessary for players, whose most common injuries, or problems, happen to their knees. Wrist guards, elbow pads, and mouth guards are always worn, too.

RISK FACTOR

Roller Derby teams wear team shirts and tight shorts or pants. They're often in bright colors and shiny **fabrics**, and they sometimes paint their faces!

RENAME YOURSELF

Most players take on a special name when they play Roller Derby. Some names tell that a person is superfast or a good hitter. They're often a play on a saying or famous person's name. Only one person can have that name!

RISK FACTOR

Roller Derby players are quite fit. They're able to skate fast and be **aggressive** on the track. Perhaps their most important skill is falling safely!

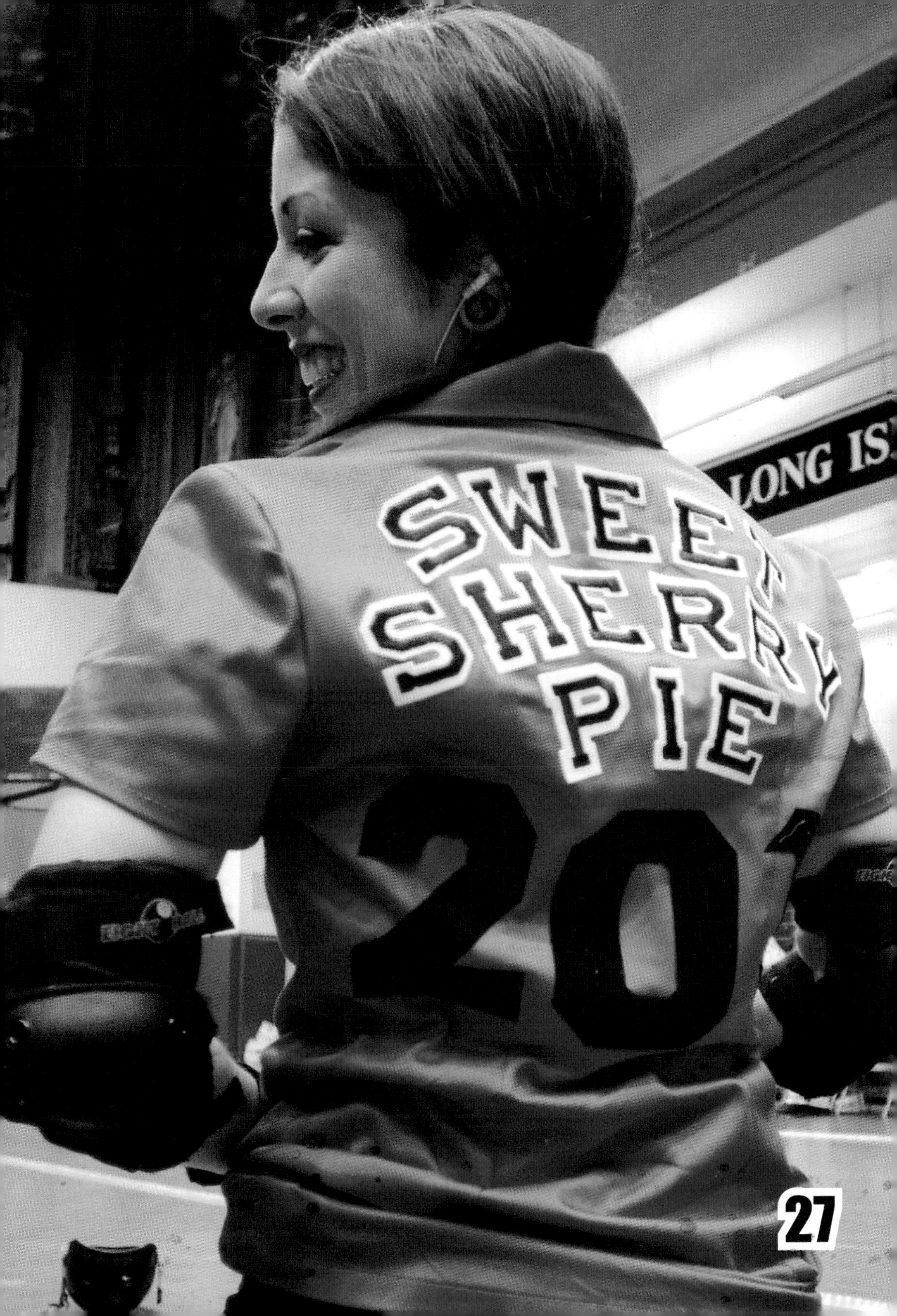
LONG IS
SWEET
SHERRY
PIE
20

A TEAM EFFORT

Roller Derby teams are often started and run by the players. They train together, working on Roller Derby skills and getting stronger for their sport. While the bouts take a lot of effort, Roller Derby teams are full of friendship and fun!

RISK FACTOR

Skaters need to be able to start and stop skating quickly and get around other players. They practice a lot to do this well!

ROLLER DERBY SAFETY TIPS

- Wear all proper safety gear, including a helmet, kneepads, elbow pads, wrist guards, and a mouth guard.

- Keep skates in good working order.

- Stay fit in other ways so you can keep up in a jam.

- Take care of any bruises or pain after a practice or bout.

- Learn how to fall safely.

- Never block other players from behind or use your elbows above shoulder height.

FOR MORE INFORMATION

BOOKS

Hamilton, John. *Inline Skating*. Minneapolis, MN: ABDO Publishing Co., 2014.

Jamieson, Victoria. *Roller Girl*. New York, NY: Dial Books, 2015.

WEBSITES

Junior Roller Derby Association
www.juniorrollerderby.org/home.php
Learn more about Roller Derby you can try right now!

The Rules of Flat Track Roller Derby
www.wftda.com/rules/20141201
Check out the rules of Roller Derby so you can be ready to skate.

GLOSSARY

aggressive: acting with forceful energy and purpose

event: a happening

fabric: a kind of cloth

foul: a breaking of the rules

league: a group of sports teams that face each other

pace: to set the speed of

referee: someone who makes sure players follow the rules

INDEX